HOW TO WRITE A BOOK REVIEW

An easy-to-learn template for writing book reviews and discussion guides

By Sarah S. Davis

a Broke by Books production

How to Write a Book Review
Published by Broke by Books Productions
Swarthmore, Pennsylvania

www.brokebybooks.com

First Edition © 2020 Sarah S. Davis

A version of the *City of Girls* book discussion guide was published on Book Riot on January 9th, 2020. Copyright © 2020 Sarah S. Davis

All rights reserved. No portion of this book may be reproduced in any form without permission from the publisher, except as permitted by U.S. copyright law. For permissions contact: sarahsdaviswrites@gmail.com

Cover by Sarah S. Davis

TABLE OF CONTENTS

Dedication 1

Chapter One: Introduction 3

Chapter Two: Crash Course in Writing Book Reviews............ 9

Chapter Three: Introducing the Template 19

Chapter Four: Part 1: Introduction... 25

Chapter Five: Part 2: Summary and Key Takeaways 29

Chapter Six: Part 3: Discussion Questions (optional)............... 36

Chapter Seven: Part 4: Quotes (Optional) 39

Chapter Eight: Part 5: Pros and Cons 43

Chapter Nine: Part 6: Overall Assessment 50

Chapter Ten: Part 7: Similar Books (Optional) 54

Chapter Eleven: Part 8: Further Information............................ 58

Chapter Twelve: Congrats!.. 62

Appendix A: Completed Book Discussion Guide Review for *City of Girls* 63

Appendix B: Completed Book Review for *Why Fish Don't Exist*... 75

Appendix C: 30 Book Discussion Questions 81

Bonus: How to Recommend Books: A Crash Course in Reader's Advisory... 84

Bonus: 20 Bookish Websites to Find Your Next Read 92

Acknowledgments 107

About the Author 108

Other Books by This Author 109

DEDICATION

To the librarians out there making life magical.

CHAPTER ONE:
INTRODUCTION

If you've found your way to this book, chances are you want to start reviewing books but are unsure of where to start.

Maybe you feel intimidated by book reviews, perhaps by bad memories of writing book reports for school.

You might feel like you need to live up to a *New York Times Book Review* level of criticism in order to write a good book review.

But what's really holding you back?

I'm guessing it's fear.

Yep, we've all had it... fear of failing to write a good book review.

I've been there.

In my earliest professional book reviews, I doubted myself the night before deadline... who was *I* to be judging this book? Where would I find the *confidence* to be a book reviewer? What if I was wrong, and the book was actually great? What if I said it was fantastic, but every other review out there disagreed?

It all boiled down to one thing in those earliest days in my book reviewing career:

- A fear of my own voice and authority as a book reviewer because I lacked a grasp on book reviewing basics.

And if you're anything like me, you're also plagued with self-doubt when it comes to reviewing books.

So here's your pep talk…

Let's get one thing clear:

You, **yes,** *you* can write a great review of any book *without fear*.

This guide is designed to help you grow into a confident book reviewer ready to tackle the task no matter your qualifications.

To do so, we'll use a template you can adapt for any book review or grow into a book discussion guide.

First, Hi! I'm Sarah, and I'm Your Host

You might be wondering, who am I, Sarah S. Davis, to be writing this guide to reviewing books?

Well, books are simply the core of my existence. Yes, I love reading books, but I also interact with them every day as an author, book journalist, librarian, and book blogger. Books are my bread and butter, my passion for living.

My experience in publishing goes back more than a decade and really started taking off after I became a book reviewer for Kirkus Reviews. I wrote reviews for nonfiction and fiction books alike at Kirkus both in their Kirkus Indie division and in the main Fiction section. I've also written book reviews for PsychCentral.

I have a deep knowledge of writing book discussion guides and study guides for BookRags, EBSCO's NoveList, and Instaread. I also served as a study guide editor at BookRags.

I've also written feature articles for Audible, Penguin Random House, Electric Literature, and Book Riot. Besides contributing more than 100 articles for Book Riot, I've also worked as a Bibliologist recommending books to customers for over two years.

I manage Broke by Books, a book blog I've successfully monetized over six years.

And last but not least, I'm the #1 bestselling author of several books about books, including _A Reader's Library of Book Quotes_ and _The Great Literature Trivia Quiz Book_.

Together, this experience makes me feel confident that I can teach you how to write book reviews.

This Book's Audience

This book about how to write book reviews is designed primarily for:

- Bloggers seeking to write book reviews on their blogs.
- Video bloggers looking to develop a transcript for their video book review.
- Students, including high school and college age, completing a book review assignment.
- People who write reviews on Amazon and/or Goodreads seeking to grasp the basics of reviewing books.

To do so, we will go through each component in the core book review template step by step.

Example Texts

For this guide, we will assemble book reviews for two different books using the review model:

- The historical fiction novel *City of Girls* (2019) by Elizabeth Gilbert, and:
- The memoir and science nonfiction book *Why Fish Don't Exist* (2020) by Lulu Miller

After each section, we'll check in with the book reviews we are building for these two books. And in Appendix A and Appendix B, respectively, you can check out the complete book reviews for these books. That way you can see what they look like as finished products.

It isn't necessary for you to have read these books; although for the purposes of this guide, there will be spoilers for both books. Still, *City of Girls* and *Why Fish Don't Exist* are five-star reads in their own right so I encourage you to check them out!

Follow Along: Practice Makes Perfect!

I suggest you go through the process of writing a book review while you work your way through the book.

It's up to you if you want to start fresh with a book you're reading now or are about to finish — or if you'd like to focus on a book you've already read.

Sometimes it can be helpful to learn something new starting fresh, but it's also the case that starting with a book you're already deeply familiar with can have its advantages, too.

Learning Objectives

Here are some of our main learning objectives for this guide book.

After reading *How to Write a Book Review* and practicing the exercises you'll:

- Establish your authority as a book reader and book reviewer.
- Go beyond a simple star rating system to dig into the meaty substance of a book—and no, you don't need an English literature degree to do it.
- Learn a simple book review template you can use with any book.
- Understand how to take your book review up a notch and write a discussion guide that will rank high in searches.

By the last page of this guide, you'll have a firm grip on book reviewing.

Bonus Material!

I'm also including two bonuses in this book.

First, you'll find a crash course in recommending books. The art and science of recommending books is called reader's advisory, and in this bonus chapter you'll learn how to do it. Reader's advisory shares some qualities with book reviewing. If you enjoy reviewing books, I have a hunch you'll like learning about how to take it the next step further and personally recommend great books to other readers.

Second, you've got a massive, TBR-busting list of more than 20 book websites for every niche and every interest. With this bonus list, you'll never run out of places to find awesome book content.

No Panic Necessary

If you're feeling overwhelmed by all this, please don't worry!

This book is structured so you can easily pick it up, work through the template, plug it in, and go. I do hope you'll stick around, though, to learn more about taking a book review higher, from basic to brilliant.

Sound like a five-star kind of book?

Let's get started!

Sarah S. Davis, M.S.L.S.

June 2020

CHAPTER TWO:

CRASH COURSE IN WRITING BOOK REVIEWS

What is the actual purpose of a book review?

This seems like such a basic question until you begin to unpack it. Let's get to thinking about it more. Because in order to write a great book review, you need to have a philosophy on what you want your book reviews to achieve.

Let's talk about what a helpful book review does:

- ★ Summarizes the key positives and negatives about a book.
- ★ Delivers an overall assessment of a book's merits.
- ★ Provides necessary background information about the book.
- ★ Contextualizes the book's noteworthiness.
- ★ Includes resources for further information.

Let's talk about what an unhelpful review does:

- → Critiques the author on a personal level.
- → Fails to support the review's critical analysis with quotes and examples.
- → Struggles to balance the reviewer's personal reaction with objectivity.
- → Lacks precise language and instead uses vague reaction words.

→ Criticizes the shopping experience outside the author's control (e.g. late shipping).

You'll notice that so far we have placed a great deal of emphasis on books being *helpful* or *unhelpful*. That's because *book reviews are designed to be resources*. These resources help other people make consumer decisions to obtain the book and read it, for themselves or for others as a gift.

The readers of your review are asking:

Is this book worth my time and money?

To that end, your book review will be a success if it helps someone answer this question, or, at a minimum, if they should add the books as "To-Read" on Goodreads or place a hold request with the library. It's important to note that a book review that is positive about a book is just as helpful as a negative review. Helping someone choose to skip reading a book is equally important as helping them decide to buy the book.

Your personal philosophy for writing book reviews will reflect your answer. But the key takeaway here is that a successful book review is a resource for helping others. It is *not* to be buried under your heavily personalized emotional reaction. If you write with that purpose, you'll never stray far from penning a good book review.

More on that in a little bit…

For the rest of this chapter, we will help you find your confidence to write book reviews by arming you with ammo for distilling what to look for when you read a book you want to review. Then we'll look at how to prep and be productive before and during your book review process. You'll get my special **A Better Critique: ABC's of Book Reviewing Chart**. And then we'll spend some time answering some FAQs about book reviewing. By the time we wrap this chapter up, you'll be all set and ready to go dive into the template and start reviewing.

Let's get started!

How to Prep for Your Book Review

If you're set on reviewing a particular book, there are ways to prep and be productive from the beginning.

1. **Go into it blind:** Don't read other reviews of the book before you begin. This will ensure that your critical take remains pure and devoid of influence.

2. **Take notes:** Get ready to mark the book up! On a digital copy, add notes and make highlights. If you're reading an eBook, you can write your thoughts on private status updates and notes on Goodreads to review later. Of course, if you're reading a book on paper, you can add margin notes, underlines, highlights… or keep things clean and just include sticky notes. This process of annotation is called *glossing* a book.

3. **Quarantine your reaction for 24 hours:** I always advocate waiting at least 24 hours after you've finished a book before you start drafting a review. Why? How many times have we all read a book, saw a movie, or watched a TV series finale and felt a burning flame of emotion that faded after time? **Your "hot take" immediately after finishing the book might change with time, so don't base your**

review on it. I know I'm prone to judging a film right after I see it but later cool off once I've had some space to reflect.

Take quotes like a beast...

Of all the components of a book to take note of, quotes are really the most important ammo to support your book review.

If you're wondering what kinds of quotes to look out for, be sure to choose ones that you find particularly memorable. For instance, definitely highlight quotes that:

- Inspire intense emotions.
- You disagree with.
- Teach you something new.
- Read like a thesis statement.
- Contain a character or the author's epiphany or moment of change.
- Include important facts and figures.
- Repeat again and again.

As stated earlier, you can highlight quotes, add bookmarks, and leave private notes in an eBook. With a paper copy, you can note a quotation however you see fit.

Unsubstantiated and vague book reviews often lack primary supporting evidence like this. Quotes are so important to a successful book review because they back your opinions and personal reactions up with textual evidence.

Now you know to use quotes, but what else should you look for when writing a book?

Introducing: A Better Critique: The ABC's of Book Reviewing!

I created this alphabet of book reviewing for this guide. Each of the 26 letters of the alphabet represents a factor you could consider when shaping your book review. From **Ask** to **Zesty**, I guarantee you'll find at least a few questions that will spark critical thought to help you get brainstorming for your book review.

A Better Critique: The Book Reviewing Alphabet

For generating ideas and critical thinking about books

Ask - What questions did the book leave you with?

Brevity - Is the book too short? Too long?

Craft - What can you learn from the author's writing craft techniques?

Debut - Is this the author's debut? If so, how do they do with their first book?

Expertise - Does this author display a certain kind of authority or expertise for the subject matter?

Fresh - Does the author bring a fresh take to the subject matter?

Gab - What is the dialogue like in the book?

Hero / Heroine - How does the hero or heroine evolve during the book?

Information - How does the author handle introducing background information (expository information) in the book?

Journey - Evaluate the journey of the hero or heroine throughout the story.

Key Takeaways - What are the key takeaways you've gotten from the book?

Learn - What did you learn from the book?

Mood - What's the mood of the book? For example, a sober vs. a light-hearted mood.

Narrator - How does the narrator—or lack thereof—affect the reading experience?

Originality - How original and creative is the book and the author's take on the subject matter?

Pacing - How well is the story paced? For example, is it a page-turner you can't put down or more of a slog?

Quotes - Analyze a few major quotes from the book.

Realistic - Is the story realistic?

Symbols - What symbols occurred in the book?

Themes - What major themes does the book grapple with?

Unique - What makes this book unique?

Voice - What is the voice of the book like?

Wonder - Does the book leave you with a sense of astonishment and wonder?

X-ray - How does the author layer multiple themes, storylines, symbols, etc. in the book?

Yawn - Is the book boring or dull?

Zesty - Is the prose lively and entertaining or dense and heavy?

After you've gone through the book reviewing alphabet, let's wrap this chapter up with a few FAQs about writing book reviews. Then you can launch into the template in Chapter Three and get going on your review.

Frequently Asked Questions about Book Reviews and Book Reviewing

Let's start by dismantling some common misbeliefs about book reviewing. You yourself might be asking these questions:

- Don't you have to be a professional book critic in order to write a satisfying book review?
- Aren't book reviews really intimidating?
- Do you have to have academic or work credentials before you can write book reviews?

The answers to all of *these* questions are a firm: *"No!"*

But… you may also be wondering:

- Do book reviews matter?
- Can anyone write a book review?
- Do book reviews still get traffic for websites?

The answers to all of these questions is a resounding: *"Yes!"*

I start with these basic misconceptions about book reviewing to soothe your nerves about writing book reviews. The truth is, anyone can review a book, including you, and create a helpful resource for writers.

Answers to Common Questions about Book Reviewing

Q: But I'm not an expert!

A: Reviewing a fantasy novel set in a wondrous land you'll never visit?

Trying to craft a review on a technical subject unfamiliar to you?

Writing a book review in a genre you're not very familiar with?

Evaluating a book whose narrator is a different gender identity?

At first, all these situations sound nerve-wracking! Don't you have to be an authority in order to review books in those scenarios?

Good new, dear reader: you're *always* an expert…for two reasons:

1. Because you are writing from the perspective of someone who has read the book at hand. As soon as you finish reading the book, you're an expert on the book at hand. So know you've got this.
2. You know what it's like to be a reader. You bring your knowledge and experience of being a reader to this specific book.

Q: Should I write my review in the first person or third?

A: I was trained to write book reviews for Kirkus Reviews, which, like Publishers Weekly, The Horn Book, and other established book review publications, are not narrated in first person. I refer to these reviews as "ghost reviews" because the author of the review is anonymous and, therefore, never revealed.

For a few years, I stuck to this format even on my own personal blog because I felt it was essential. But gradually, I introduced more of my take on the books I'm reviewing and writing about. In the end, I've found a balance between highly personal reviews of books that I have a strong reaction to on an emotional, cognitive, or craft level and more straightforward ghost reviews.

In my experience, readers of book reviews react most strongly to book reviews that include at least a little bit of the reviewer in the article. Your distinct voice and perspective is effective because people learn that a book affected you on some emotional level. People are curious about books that move us either positively or negatively.

At the end of the day, they want to know how a book made you feel. Incorporate your feelings and reactions, but remember: you're reviewing a book, not your feelings.

Q: Should I use a star rating system?

A: It's up to you! Personally, I usually only rate books with star ratings on Goodreads. By writing discussion guide-review hybrids, I'm implying that I enjoyed reading the book enough to go to the trouble to make a guide for it. But it can be super fun to rate a book on various factors you include with rating systems. My advice is to try what works for you.

Q: Do I need to review every book or review copy I read?

A: No! You are under no obligation to review a book you received as an ARC (Advanced Review Copy, sometimes called an eARC for digital copies). Never promise a review and never feel trapped into writing a review.

In fact, from a book blogging perspective, I would strongly suggest *not* reviewing every ARC you get. That's because ARCs are often given out to the same bloggers, so you'll end up duplicating reviews of the same midlist titles.

My strategy? Go big or go home: write discussion guides-reviews for the books that make book club lists, like those run by Reese Witherspoon and Oprah. You're far more likely to get meaningful traffic for the buzzy books than for midlist titles that no one is actually reading beyond bloggers in the ARC circuit.

All right, now that we have those FAQs answered, let's get onto the actual book review template!

CHAPTER THREE:
INTRODUCING THE TEMPLATE

Your template for a book review and why it works!

Unsure how to structure your book review? Look no further. I'm sharing with you my tried-and-true template for crafting a substantive, helpful book review.

Each of these components serve a purpose. I've learned over the years through SEO optimization and keyword research that these components of a book that readers look for the most.

Here's the template:

Part 1: Introduce the book and the author

- Include any background you can find about the book.
- Briefly summarize the author's biography.

Part 2: Plot Summary

- If you're writing a review that must include all aspects of the plot, be sure to include a spoiler warning.
- Summarize the plot in no more than 3-5 paragraphs.
- Add 3-5 key takeaways (for nonfiction only).

Part 3: Discussion Questions (Optional)

- Include 5-10 discussion questions.

Part 4: Quotes (Optional)

- Include 5-10 key quotes from the book with page numbers

Part 5: Pros and Cons

- Include 2-4 positive qualities or "Pros" of the book as bullet points (or plus signs).
- Include 2-4 negative qualities or "Cons" of the book as bullet points (or negative signs).
- Depending on whether your review is positive or negative, the balance between the pros and cons will be weighted differently.

Part 6: Overall Assessment

- Synthesise the points you make in Part 3. Ultimately, does the book get a favorable review?

Part 7: Similar Books (Optional)

- Include 3-5 similar books.

Part 8: Further Information

- Include the stats of the book: pub date, publisher, page count
- Link to other resources: author interviews, reviews on authority sites.

You'll notice that **Part 3 (Discussion Questions), Part 4 (Quotes),** and **Part 6 (Similar Books)** are optional. That's because the full format of this book review template actually covers the scope of not only a book review, but a book discussion guide as well.

Writing Discussion Guide-Reviews

Wait a second—you may be saying—isn't this a book about how to write book *reviews*, not book discussion guides?

My answer to you would be... it's a two-in-one!

The fact is, as I've mined my own traffic and data over the years, book discussion guides (also known alternatively as book group guides, book club guides, study guides, or reading group guides) bring in the most consistent traffic to my site vs. traditional book reviews.

The traditional book review includes all the parts above except for Discussion Questions, Quotes, and Similar Books. You can read this guide and follow that template for a successful book review. We will be using this basic book review template for a book review of the nonfiction book *Why Fish Don't Exist* (2020) by Lulu Miller.

Or you can push it a little further with more book discussion guide content people are actually searching for online.

Take a look at the search traffic for *City of Girls*, the novel we will be using in this book as we work through the parts of a book review. Courtesy of the Chrome extension Keywords Everywhere, we can see what people look for when you search Google for: "city of girls":

Related Keywords　　　　　　　　　　　Export to CSV

Keyword	Vol	CPC	Comp	Trend
city of girls review	4,400	$0.01	0.01	
city of girls summary	1,300	$0.25	0.02	
city of girls kindle	140	$0.03	0.4	
books like city of girls	140	$0.38	0.27	
city of girls movie	0	$0.00	0	
city of girls characters	0	$0.00	0	
city of girls wiki	0	$0.00	0	
city of girls book club questions	0	$0.00	0	
city of girls quotes	0	$0.00	0	
city of girls audiobook	0	$0.00	0	

You can see here how people are searching not just for reviews, but for the kind of content you'll find in a typical book discussion guide: summary, characters, book club questions, and quotes. This means you can easily up your traffic by providing just two more components: Discussion Questions and Similar Books.

And you'll see that book discussion guides make up a substantial amount of traffic, with a recent guide for Rebecca Serle's *In Five Years* ranking fourth and Jenny Offil's *Weather* getting hits near the top, too:

Top Posts for 30 days ending 2020-06-09 (Summarized)	
7 Days	**30 Days**	Quarter	Year	All time	
May 10, 2020 to Today	
Title	**Views**
Take the Ultimate Children's Literature Trivia Quiz	4,082
The 15 Best Tarot Books: from Beginner to Advanced	2,209
15 Best Books with Happy Endings	1,026
Book Group Guide for IN FIVE YEARS: Questions, Ending Explained & Similar Books	840
The 25 Best Quotes from THE GOLDFINCH	668
The Word Count of 175 Favorite Novels	643
10 Terrific Short Story Collections for Kids	525
Top 50 Literature Trivia Quiz Questions	407
10 Essential Mystery Short Story Anthologies	398
The 30 Best Quotes from "Peter Pan"	333
Home page / Archives	280
10 Best YA Short Story Anthologies	243
Brothers and Sisters in Fiction: Great Siblings of Literature and Fiction	230
10 Discussion Questions for WEATHER by Jenny Offill	146

This shows how book discussion guides trending in search traffic. If you're already writing a review, adding in a few extra features can see your readership increase.

Throughout this book, we will be going step by step through the components of a discussion guide-review hybrid for Elizabeth Gilbert's *City of Girls*. You can find the complete product in Appendix A. Study the guide's components as the book goes on and refer back to the finished example in Appendix A to see what it all looks like together.

On the other hand, you can read a book review with just the core components in the review for *Why Fish Don't Exist*, compiled in Appendix B.

Other Book Discussion Guide Components: Sometimes book discussion guides also include sections like Themed Book Group Ideas. I'm not including those here because they are not essential to a book discussion guide, but feel free to add these sections into your product.

Learn as you go

Reader, I suggest starting off with the basic book review template before diving into writing discussion guides, but I wanted to teach you both book reviews and their cousin, reading group guides, in one easy-to-follow manual: the one you're reading right now.

I recommend choosing a book that you're about to read or have recently finished and going through this guide's template, completing each step as you go.

CHAPTER FOUR:

PART 1: INTRODUCTION

The Template

- Include any background you can find about the book.
- Briefly summarize the author's biography.

How to Write the Introduction Section

In the opening section of the book review, you'll want to give a little background about the book you are reviewing. In 1-3 paragraphs, provide some context for the book and introduce the author.

For example, you might want to include the following details about the book:

- Where the book fits in its genre or subject—is it a noteworthy self-help book or genre-bending sci-fi novel?
- Any "buzz" around the book—is it highly anticipated? Has it made a lot of Best of the Month lists?
- Has the book been chosen for a national book club—was it selected for Oprah's Book Club or Book of the Month Club?

Fit these facts inside a paragraph about the author:

- The author's full name (or pen name).
- The author's previous books—or note if it's a debut.

- Magazines, newspapers, and websites the author has written for.
- Unique credentials for writing this book.

Example: Introduction for *City of Girls*

Elizabeth Gilbert, best known for her memoir *Eat, Pray, Love* (2006) and self-help book *Big Magic* (2015), returns to fiction with *City of Girls* (June 4, 2019, Riverhead). This epic historical novel is told from the perspective of Vivian Morris, who moves to New York City when she is nineteen. Vivian finds community living in her bohemian Aunt Peg's midtown theater. But Vivian makes a crucial mistake that shatters her new life just as America enters the Second World War. *City of Girls* has received much acclaim. The novel was chosen as [Amazon's Best Book of the Year So Far in June 2019](#) and was nominated for a Goodreads Choice Award for Historical Fiction (2019). [The film rights](#) have also been purchased.

Introduction to *Why Fish Don't Exist*

NPR science reporter and podcaster Lulu Miller offers an eye-opening look at the way nature connects us all in *Why Fish Don't Exist: A Story of Loss, Love, and the Hidden Order of Life* (April 14, 2020, Simon & Schuster), her first book. Miller focuses on David Starr Jordan (1851-1931), a leading ichthyologist who specialized in fish taxonomy. Miller weaves Jordan's story of resilience after setbacks along with her own personal struggles following challenges. Along the way, Miller scrutinizes Jordan and re-evaluates her hero worship for the influential scientist, who played a substantial part in the eugenics movement in America. Ultimately, in trying to find order in her personal chaos, Miller delivers novel ways to see our natural world.

CHAPTER FIVE:

PART 2: SUMMARY AND KEY TAKEAWAYS

The Template

- If you're writing a review that must include all aspects of the plot, be sure to include a spoiler warning.
- Summarize the plot in no more than 3-5 paragraphs.
- If reviewing a nonfiction book, add 3-5 key takeaways.

How to Write the Summary Section

Next up, we have the summary. This part is pretty straightforward, but it's an essential component of the book review that shouldn't be glossed over or omitted. You'll find that many readers searching for a book review are primarily searching for a summary.

You're going to need to make a decision on two factors:

- Are you going to summarize the plot and include spoilers? If yes, you'll want to preface this section with a spoiler alert: **"This plot summary contains spoilers."** If your whole review or guide contains spoiler, you'll want to front load the warning: **"This review contains spoilers"** or **"This book discussion guide contains spoilers."**

And:

- Will you summarize the whole book or just include an overview? Summarizing the whole book should take up no more than 3-5 paragraphs top while an overview is typically just a paragraph or two and is similar in length to the kind of description you might see in a book blurb.

For **fiction**, a plot summary is exactly what it says: a condensed version of the story including key plot points, the main characters, setting, and the core themes of the book. If you're writing more of a book discussion guide or book group guide, you'll want to include the full plot with spoilers.

This is also a key section for explaining the ending. Readers often search for a book on Google looking for the ending of a novel explained. Definitely include an ending analysis if you're writing a book discussion guide type of review.

For **nonfiction**, it's slightly different. To write a nonfiction summary, you'll need to simplify the book's major topics into just a few paragraphs. That doesn't mean you need to *explain* complicated concepts. Instead, you can discuss what themes make up the scope of the book.

Then, in a Key Takeaways section, extract 3-5 essential facts and conclusions and put them in bullet point form.

Example: Plot Summary for *City of Girls*
Plot Summary for *City of Girls*

This plot summary contains spoilers

In Elizabeth Gilbert's 2019 historical fiction novel, *City of Girls*, our narrator is 89-year-old Vivian Morris. In the opening pages, we learn that Vivian is writing to another woman named Angela. Vivian is attempting to answer Angela's question about who Vivian was to her late father. Vivian begins her letter in response by immersing us in her youth, starting when she moves to New York City at the age of 19 in 1940. Having been kicked out of college, Vivian lives with her bohemian Aunt Peg, who owns a vaudeville-style theater in Midtown Manhattan called the Lily Playhouse with her business and romantic partner, Olive. Vivian enjoys the glamorous life of the showgirls she befriends, in particular her roommate Celia, and experiences nights of excess, gluttony, and sexual pleasure. By day, she crafts beautiful costumes for the Lily using material from a fabric emporium where she strikes up a friendship with Marjorie, the quirky daughter of the store's owners.

As the Second World War begins to break through Vivian's sheltered life, Edna Parker Watson, an English stage actress and friend of Aunt Peg and Olive, becomes stranded in New York as England gets into the war. Aunt Peg puts on a show called "City of Girls" to feature Edna with the help of Billy, her husband who lives in L.A. "City of Girls" is a success with critics and audiences alike, and the cast and crew narrowly survives Billy's extreme behavior.

In March of 1941, tensions between Edna and her husband Arthur erupt during a fateful night, and Vivian is caught in a threesome with Arthur and Celia. Olive manages to keep Vivian's name out of the press coverage of the scandal, but the damage is done. Edna scolds Vivian, telling her she isn't an interesting woman, and Vivian flees the city, getting a ride home with her responsible Navy recruit older brother, Walter, and a fellow soldier who has a car available. On the way home, Walter lectures Vivian, and the unnamed soldier calls her a "dirty little whore," a remark that fills Vivian with shame and self-hatred as she lives at home with her parents in a state of depression. Vivian escapes a marriage to Jim Larsen, an employee at her father's company, because Jim enlists in the military after the Pearl Harbor attacks in December 1941.

Vivian senses that she's dodged a bullet and a life of unhappiness with Jim. When Aunt Peg drives up to her parents' house and asks Vivian to return to the city in the summer of 1942, Vivian eagerly hears her out. Aunt Peg's been commissioned to put on shows at the Brooklyn Navy Yard and needs a costume designer. Vivian agrees and, with delight, moves back to the Lily. Life has changed, with Edna on Broadway, Celia gone, and Billy elsewhere. Vivian dives headfirst into the creative obstacle of creating costumes despite war shortages. Vivian is distraught when she finds out Walter died on a ship in the Pacific.

After the war, Vivian and Marjorie purchase a house and set up a bridal gown boutique. Marjorie has a son who Vivian helps to raise, and Vivian finds sexual satisfaction in multiple male partners, though never a lasting relationship. When the Brooklyn Navy Yard is set to be formally closed down in 1965, Aunt Peg is asked to put on one last show. Since Peg is too weak from illness, Vivian agrees to take on the project. After the performance, a scarred police officer comes up to her and makes a stunning confession: he was the soldier who drove her to her parents' house and judged her to be a "dirty little whore." The man's name is Frank and he unsuccessfully attempts to apologize for the regretful words that have haunted him since, Vivian shuts him down and leaves. Seeking sympathy from Aunt Peg, Vivian is surprised when Peg expresses disappointment in her. Olive tells Vivian she needs to stand in the "field of honor" and take the high ground. After much deliberation, Vivian reaches out to Frank. Together, they strike up an unusual friendship that borders on a platonic romance. Since Frank's PTSD makes him uncomfortable inside and can't bear physical touch, they walk through the city during long nights. Vivian helps him process some of his trauma. He eventually introduces her to his daughter, Angela, the woman to whom Vivian is writing. Vivian designs Angela's wedding gown in 1971. Frank dies of sudden illness in 1977. When Angela writes to Vivian, it's to tell her that her mother has passed away and that she was always curious about Vivian's close relationship with Frank. In closing, Vivian offers her friendship to Angela, looking back on her long and mostly happy life with extraordinary women.

Example: Summary and Key Takeaways of *Why Fish Don't Exist*

Lulu Miller opens her book *Why Fish Don't Exist* with a tantalizing question: how did scientist and educator David Starr Jordan (1851-1931) find the resilience to pick up and keep going after the 1906 San Francisco Earthquake destroyed his life's work?

And so kicks off Miller's debut as she introduces her personal story into her biography of Jordan. Jordan's courage to continue on after the earthquake smashed thousands of his fish samples was extraordinarily appealing to Miller, all the more so because the natural disaster shattered the glass specimen jars, leaving the fish unidentified.

As the book goes on, Miller summarizes Jordan's life and work as she fleshes out her own story. Miller struggled with depression over the years and clung to Jordan as an example of finding the courage to go on. But the more Miller investigates Jordan, the more complicated her relationship to him becomes as she learns the extent to Jordan's power. In particular, Miller unveils how influential Jordan was in the American eugenics movement and dangles a tantalizing rumor that he might have murdered Jane Stanford with poison.

Miller asks readers to question everything we know about nature and the hierarchies in life in her closing pages, challenging us to rethink the taxonomies that can be so harmful. Miller's life story, initially introduced to frame Jordan's biography, eventually emerges as the dominant narrative. Miller invites readers into her life as she heals from depression and finds self-acceptance and love.

Key Takeaways

- David Starr Jordan (1851-1931)was an influential naturalist and educator who specialized in ichthyology, the study of fish. Jordan was responsible for discovering thousands of fish, over a fifth of all fish species in his lifetime.
- Jordan might have been involved with the murder of Jane Stanford, the co-founder of Stanford University where Jordan served as president.
- Jordan endorsed the eugenics movement and was responsible for its spread in America, which led to thousands of government-sanctioned sterilizations.
- The theory that "fish" don't exist belongs to cladists, whose classification system is based on evolution. The cladists allege that the category of "fish" actually belongs to several different types of creatures since life evolved out of the ocean, so "fish" as we know it, encompass too many different species who eventually evolved.
- *Why Fish Don't Exist* is the debut book by Lulu Miller is a science journalist who has written with NPR and other publications like *The New Yorker*.

CHAPTER SIX:

PART 3: DISCUSSION QUESTIONS (OPTIONAL)

The Template

- Include 5-10 discussion questions

How to Write the Discussion Questions Section

In this section, you can write about 5-10 specific questions tailored to the book you're reading. Though I've labeled it an optional section, there are many advantages to including discussion questions along with your review.

Discussion questions are a key component of any book club or reading group guide. Over the years, I've found that my free book discussion guides / hybrid book reviews see a steady current of traffic.

If you're not sure where to begin, check out Appendix C, which contains 30 general book discussion questions that work for most books. You can choose which ones you like and adapt them to your review.

Example: Discussion Questions for *City of Girls*

1. *City of Girls* takes its title from the name of a play that the Lily puts on to great success. How do you interpret the title as a larger theme in Gilbert's book?
2. How does Vivian's late grandmother influence the woman Vivian becomes?
3. In many ways, Vivian's life is driven by a desire for pleasure. What are the potential consequences and dangers she faces in her pursuit for pleasure? How is her unconventional drive for pleasure indicative of the wider trends of liberation for women during the century?
4. Why does Vivian participate in the threesome? What events drive her to such a betrayal?
5. Discuss the theme of shame and gender in *City of Girls*. How does Frank's dismissal of Vivian as a "dirty little whore" inform Vivian's personal sense of shame? How do her views change over time?
6. How does the war give Vivian a sense of perspective? In particular, how does her brother Walter's death affect Vivian?
7. Define Olive's "field of honor" concept. How is Vivian's willingness to stand in the field of honor a rite of passage? How is her character different before and after doing so?
8. Discuss Vivian's evolving definition of emotional and physical intimacy. How do her earliest romantic and sexual relationships compare to her later relationship with Frank?
9. Vivian, her friends, and her colleagues embrace a radically unconventional lifestyle far ahead of their time. Vivian notes to Angela: "With the greatest of pride, I was

able to look out across all the cultural upheavals and transformations of the 1960s, and know this: *My people got there first*" (p. 470). Discuss some of the ways that Vivian and her allies anticipated the century's revolutionary changes.
10. Vivian places a great deal of importance on female friendship and closes her narrative by offering friendship to Angela. Compare and contrast the friendships she has with women over the years.

CHAPTER SEVEN:

PART 4: QUOTES (OPTIONAL)

The Template

- Include 5-10 meaningful quotes from the book with page numbers

How to Write the Quotes Section

Adding quotes is another optional component of a book review or book discussion guide. All you have to do is list 5-10 quotes from the book that you felt warrant special attention, along with page count. As you read, make notation of quotes that stay with you or resonate in some way.

The best kind of quotes to include are:

- Though-provoking
- Wise
- Debatable
- Important to the book's themes
- Emotionally resonant

If you're stumped on finding quotes, check out the Goodreads page for a book. There's always a quotes section that aggregates quotes that people have voted on to be the most popular. If you just finished the book and need a little refresher, start here.

You might also want to go so far as to analyze each quote, but it's not necessary. Readers are mainly looking for quotes that spark discussion for book clubs with these kinds of quote roundups.

You could also break this out into a separate post. My post of the best quotes from Donna Tartt's *The Goldfinch* gets traffic every day from Google and Pinterest even though I published it years ago. People are hungry for book quotes, as *A Reader's Library of Book Quotes*, my bestselling book that collects quotes about books, certainly demonstrates.

Example: Quotes from *City of Girls*

- "She was of the mind that people should make their own decisions about their own lives, if you can imagine such a preposterous thing!" — Vivian (referencing Peg), page 45
- "I hope you're having a good time, too. People will tell you not to waste your youth having too much fun, but they're wrong. Youth is an irreplaceable treasure, and the only respectable thing to do with irreplaceable treasure is to waste it. So do the right thing with your youth, Vivian — squander it." — Billy, page 152
- "'*Hush,*' she said. "I'm thinking at the top of my lungs." — Peg, page 157
- "In my experience, this is the hardest lesson of them all. After a certain age, we are all walking around this world in bodies made of secrets and shame and sorrow and old, unhealed injuries. Our hearts grow sore and misshapen around all this pain - yet somehow, still, we carry on." — Vivian, page 342
- "Resist change at your own peril, Vivian. When something ends, let it end." — Peg, page 353
- "Anyway, at some point in a woman's life, she just gets tired of being ashamed all the time." — Vivian, page 377
- "The field of honor is a painful field...(It) is not a place where children can play. Children don't have any honor, you see, and they aren't expected to, because it's too difficult for them. It's too painful. But to become an adult, one must step into the field of honor. Everything will be expected of you now. You will need to be vigilant in your principles. Sacrifices will be demanded. You will be judged. If you make mistakes, you must account for

them. There will be instances when you must cast aside your impulses and take a higher stance than another person - a person without honor - might take. Such an instance may hurt, but that's why honor is a painful field." — Olive, page 405

- "The world ain't straight. You grow up thinking things are a certain way. You think there are rules. You think there's a way that things have to be. You try to live straight. But the world doesn't care about your rules, or what you believe. The world ain't straight, Vivian. Never will be. Our rules, they don't mean a thing. The world just happens to you sometimes, is what I think. And people just gotta keep moving through it, best they can." — Frank, page 428

CHAPTER EIGHT:
PART 5: PROS AND CONS

The Template

- Include 1-4 positive qualities of the book as bullet points (or plus signs)
- Include 1-4 negative qualities of the book as bullet points (or negative signs)
- Depending on whether your review is positive or negative, the balance between the pros and cons will be weighted differently. A book that is more recommendable will have more pros while a book you have more misgivings about will have more cons.

How to Write the Pros and Cons Section

Next we have the Pros and Cons section of the review. Perhaps more than any other section of the review, readers are looking for the key positives and negatives of the book. This is what they've come for: validation to make a consumer decision and purchase the book. The Pros and Cons offer your expert opinion that could sway their next step—to buy or not buy.

No matter how bad a book is, you can likely find one or two positive things to say about it. Similarly, you can probably find at least one or two flaws. As review readers are looking for the objective facts when they get to the Pros and Cons section, try to keep these points general and not specific to your reading. Remember, as we go over in the Voice chapter, if you're following this guide's book review method, you're reviewing a book, not your feelings.

It's important for the Pros and Cons to be formatted in a clean, skimmable list. Nowadays straight prose reviews make for unwieldy blocks of text. Readers want you to get to the point *fast*. You'll want to separate these out and identify them as bullet points. You can customize the Pros to be plus signs (+) and the Cons to be negative signs (−), if you like. Also, you can create a variation with other names for the factors, like What Works / What Doesn't, What I Loved / What I Didn't Love, etc.

Example: Pros and Cons of *City of Girls*

Pros

Pro: Vivian's conversational, dishy narration

Vivian narrates her story with candor and a sense of intimacy with the reader. She gives herself fully, admitting her deepest mistakes and sharing gossipy rumors and facts. She has a natural talent for writing who is able to look back on her life and shape it into a story laced with suspense, intrigue, conflict, and tension. This makes the pages fly by as you can't wait to hear what she'll tell you next.

Pro: Vivian is a flawed character who feels relatable

At the story's beginning, Vivian is 19. For the first time ever, she's allowed to explore her interests and her sexuality when she moves to New York City. Anyone reading *City of Girls* can relate to Vivian for her enthusiasm and her flaws. Gilbert's novel distills our universal tendency to make mistakes. One of its core themes is youth and how being young can lead to some immature errors that are hard to let down. When she hurts, we hurt, too.

Pro: *City of Girls* is rich with historical detail

Gilbert clearly did her research. The novel is packed with historical details that make you feel immersed in Vivian's life in New York City starting in the 1940's and through the decades that follow. Yet the setting never feels like you're reading a dense history book. Instead, Gilbert makes it come alive with just enough detail to feel like you're escaping present day.

Pro: *City of Girls* is a love song to anyone who has ever felt like a misfit

One theme in *City of Girls* is how Vivian connects with other misfits. In this sense, "misfits" means anyone who doesn't conform to society's rules. Vivian doesn't fit in because she's a pleasure-seeking young woman kicked out of college with no interest in marriage. Other characters Vivian meets, including Marjorie and Aunt Peg, reject norms of gender and sexuality. Together, Vivian and her friends create a found family that thrives on love and acceptance.

Pro: The book balances fun with heavy themes

City of Girls could have been a great beach read in its own right. But Gilbert's breezy novel is elevated by sincere, thought-provoking themes. The novel deals with heavy subject matter, like shame and trauma, that linger long after the final page has been turned.

Cons

Con: The novel is almost too long

As entertaining as Vivian's narration was, the novel felt bloated at times. Gilbert could have dramatically condensed the story while at the same time, the story would have benefitted from being spread out in Vivian's life post-WWII. *City of Girls* could have stood to lose a few pages early on.

Con: The "mistake" Vivian made was not convincing

Readers start out knowing that Vivian makes a mistake that dramatically changes her life; it's right there in the book's official description. Yet the way the threesome is written is slightly confusing. Did Vivian truly want to engage in the act? Her motivations weren't quite spelled out enough to make it believable that Vivian actually wanted to partake in the ménage à trois.

Pros and Cons of *Why Fish Don't Exist*

Pros

Pro: Miller's storytelling skills make her personal narrative a satisfying read

Miller's personal character arc is set alongside Jordan's but eventually eclipses his story to tell her own. Miller is a talented storyteller who pulls us in with honesty and self-scrutiny. The ending builds towards a satisfying climax that marries Miller's personal awakening with heeder revelations about Jordan, a man she once worshipped as a hero.

Pro: *Why Fish Don't Exist* is a lively, funny trip through the science of nature

Miller manages to balance the serious subject matter with the funnier or more light-hearted passages. Miller brings a needed sense of humor to the story that spurs readers on, never dragging down the narrative.

Pro: Miller's sense of curiosity about the subject is infectious.

You might pick up Miller's book and have no idea you're looking at a delightfully entertaining story that travels through the annals of history and braids multiple subjects, like natural science, psychology, true crime. Somehow Miller manages to pull it off and craft a fascinating story.

Pro: The book is short and never dense

If you're looking for a quick nonfiction read, *Why Fish Don't Exist* is for you. At 195 pages, Miller's can be read in one big gulp or over a weekend. The story never sags but races right along with great pacing.

Pro: Kate Samworth's stunning illustrations make Miller's story come alive

Each chapter starts off with one of artist Kate Samworth's captivating illustrations for *Why Fish Don't Exist*. This exquisite artwork is worth the price of the book alone.

Cons

Con: At times, Miller's explanations of scientific beliefs can be muddled and unclear

Sometimes when Miller is explaining a complicated scientific theory or belief system, such as the fact that fish don't exist, readers might struggle to understand them. Perhaps some tables or diagrams would have helped.

CHAPTER NINE:

PART 6: OVERALL ASSESSMENT

The Template

- Synthesize the points you make in Part 3 in 1-3 paragraphs. Ultimately, does the book get a favorable review?
- End with a final assessment in one sentence.

How to Write the Overall Assessment Section

You've read the book. You've thought critically about its positives and negatives. And now you're all ready to synthesize your observations into an overall assessment.

In this space of the book, you join both your pros and cons as you weigh whether or not this book is ultimately recommendable. Sometimes you have this already worked out before you start the review. However, it's quite common to change your mind the more you write about the book throughout the course of the review. I myself have sometimes found that writing the pros and cons section can steer me into appreciating more—or less—of the book I'm recommending. Either way, by this point in the book review, you're delivering the bottom line.

In 1-3 paragraphs, tie together the pros and cons of the book and make a final argument for the book's merits or drawbacks. Your review should answer this question: "Is this book recommendable?" and, if so, "Who is this book for?" This is, in many ways, the most important section as a lot of people who click on your post will be looking for exactly this and read nothing else.

Then, after the final verdict, add a statement sentence with your bottom line.

A quick note on star ratings...

If you're an avid Goodreads reviewer, you are used to giving 1-5 stars for a book's rating.

It's up to you if you want to include a star rating for the book you're reviewing. I usually do because it's a factor that resonates with a lot of readers. If you're using a star rating system, the Overall Assessment is the place to put that.

A Note About Review Templates

If you use a review template, you might be able to program in different ratings based on factors you control. For example, you could include ratings on Characterization, Story, or World Building using a five-point scale. These ratings usually come at the end of the review here in the Overall Assessment section. The template used in this book is meant to be both general and endlessly customizable. If you're already using a review plugin or a WordPress theme's review function, feel free to adapt the Overall Assessment to your style.

Overall Assessment for *City of Girls*

Elizabeth Gilbert's *City of Girls* is epic in scope, covering a large part of the latter half of the twentieth century. The novel sweeps readers off their feet with a captivating narrator who isn't afraid to admit her blunders. Written as a letter to an old friend, *City of Girls* is told in heroine Vivian Morris's confessional style, hooking readers with her storytelling skills, flawed and relatable characters, and glamorous life.

While the story is engrossing, some parts could be condensed while others would do better to be given in more detail, in particular when she summarizes several decades in just a few pages while devoting hundreds of pages to the events of a few days. Additionally, the book could have benefited from further clarification around Vivian's motives during her mistake.

However, despite these misgivings, the novel is ultimately a success. Vivian is such an entertaining narrator and captivating character in her own right that it's hard to put the book down. It's easy to escape into Vivian's story in this character-driven historical novel that deals with topics like feminism, judgment, and youth. Just when you might think that Vivian is too frivolous a narrator, Gilbert proves that this is no gossipy book without substance. *City of Girls* rises above being just a quick beach read by handling heavy themes like trauma and shame.

Bottom Line: An unputdownable story told by a captivating, flawed character makes Elizabeth Gilbert's *City of Girls* a must-read for historical fiction fans and those who love stories with flawed-yet-relatable characters.

Overall Assessment of *Why Fish Don't Exist*

Lulu Miller's debut book *Why Fish Don't Exist* is a must-have book for anyone who likes reading about science, history, and psychology. Readers are in for a treat as Miller follows hunches and anecdotes down the rabbit hole, sparking a contagious curiosity for the subject matter in a manner similar to writers Mary Roach, Jill Lepore, and Susan Orlean. Miller mostly translates her topic well, though it can be challenging to follow at times when readers could have benefitted from more clear descriptions.

Miller's lively narrative breathes fresh scrutiny into her hero-worship for David Starr Jordan, a man whose myth she dismantles. Kate Samworth's breathtaking illustrations make this book a treasure to keep and look at again and again. Best of all, Miller successfully layers her subject and her personal story in a reckoning until they all come together in a cathartic ending.

Bottom Line: Lulu Miller's exciting debut, *Why Fish Don't Exist*, illuminates the natural order of life on our planet in this engrossing trip through science, history, and psychology threaded through with Miller's personal awakening.

CHAPTER TEN:
PART 7: SIMILAR BOOKS (OPTIONAL)

The Template

- Include 3-5 similar books.

How to Write the Similar Books Section

Why have a Similar Books section? Believe me, I can understand how it might sound excessive. But including 3-5 similar books as "Companion Reads" or "Read-a-Likes" earns the trust of your readers. Furthermore, you can gather key data based on the performance of links. You can get a better understanding of what to write next by studying your outbound traffic via the links to Goodreads and affiliate partnerships you include next to the books you recommend in this section.

Need more incentive?

A recommended reads section definitely helps you convert a free book review post into a consumer purchase by offering similar books via affiliate links. Personally, I see a fair bit of outbound link clicks to affiliate sites and Goodreads based on books I recommend at the end of my book reviews and discussion guides. You already have people on your site and they've read down to the end of your review. Don't leave that passive income opportunity on the table. Instead, include a few books you recommend for readers of the book you've reviewed.

So how to do it?

If you follow this book's method to have you actively considering similar books while you're reading, you've got a head start. But if you're truly not sure, it doesn't help to look at the "Also Boughts" and "Also Reads" section of a book's Amazon page. And if you're on Goodreads, look for the "Readers Also Enjoyed" section to the right of a book's page. Spend some time studying the algorithm for the book and pick a few that seem like solid recommendations.

Formatting Your Similar Books Section

Include the cover of a book, a brief 1-3 sentence describing what they have in common and why readers might enjoy it. Similarities could be plot, setting, genre, theme, topic, etc. Then include a link to Amazon or another retailer of your choice, plus a link to the book's page on Goodreads.

Example: Similar Books for *City of Girls*.

Dear Mrs. Bird by A.J. Pearce (2018)

City of Girls immerses readers in World War II and the mass mobilization of citizens to support the soldiers on the battlefield and those on the home front. Readers who enjoy Vivian's young perspective on the war will like A.J. Pearce's *Dear Mrs. Bird*. This novel is set in London during the early years of the war and is similarly anchored in the life of a young woman trying to make sense of the impossible conflict she and her country face.

Exit the Actress by Priya Parmar (2011)

Love the focus on drama and theater in *City of Girls*? Liked the historical setting? Try Priya Parmar's *Exit the Actress*. This novel also explores the world of acting. *Exit the Actress* is told through the eyes of Ellen "Nell" Gwyn, a real-life actress who rose to fame in Restoration England. An epistolary novel, *Exit the Actress* is told in playbills, gossip columns, diaries, letters, and more mixed formats.

Sweetbitter by Stephanie Danler (2016)

Tess, the complicated heroine of Stephanie Danler's novel *Sweetbitter*, also arrives in New York in her early adulthood. Quickly taking a job at an upscale restaurant, Tess, like Vivian in *City of Girls*, makes mistakes as she matures. One of the most palpable feelings of *City of Girls* is how it feels to be young, a quality that *Sweetbitter* shares, making it of interest for readers who were moved by Vivian's blunders and successes both.

Warlight by Michael Ondaatje (2018)

City of Girls is as much about the lingering trauma of war as it is about living in the moment of the war. Readers who were intrigued by the aftereffects of World War II will find much to like about Michael Ondaatje's *Warlight,* which is set in London immediately after the end of the military conflict. Like *City of Girls*, this engrossing novel features a young protagonist trying to make sense of his fractured life post-World War II.

CHAPTER ELEVEN:
PART 8: FURTHER INFORMATION

The Template:

- Include the stats of the book: pub date, publisher, page count
- Link to other resources: author interviews, reviews on authority sites

How to Write the Further Information Section

At long last, we've come to the end of the template… the Further Information section. I admit, before I started including this component at the end of my review, I was skeptical. But it's the librarian in me that loves to connect people to more information. Now I regularly see a lot of outbound traffic from my blog on the links that I include in a book guide or book review's Further Information section.

It really does show you're going the extra mile for your readers to do this one final step.

So what to include?

I include the cover again and provide the basic facts of the book like title, author, publication date, publisher, and page count. I also list where to buy it via an affiliate link to Amazon and also point readers to the book's Goodreads page.

I also include some combination of:

- The author's website.

- Interviews with the author.
- Video interviews with the author (search on YouTube).
- Video of the author reading the book (search on YouTube).
- Reviews from authority sites like Publishers Weekly, Kirkus Reviews, and others.

Note that you can embed the videos from YouTube into WordPress directly. Just choose the Share button and opt for the Embed function on the far left.

Example: Further Information for *City of Girls*

Loved *City of Girls*? Take your reading to another level with these resources for fans of Elizabeth Gilbert's *City of Girls*:

- Visit Elizabeth Gilbert's website
- Read an exclusive excerpt of the novel on *O the Oprah Magazine*
- Check out an interview with Gilbert about *City of Girls* and her routine
- Browse book reviews of *City of Girls* collected on Book Marks
- Watch a video of Gilbert being interviewed about the novel

The Stats:

City of Girls by Elizabeth Gilbert
Published June 9th, 2020 by Riverhead (Penguin Random house)
480 pages (hardcover)

Where to Find It:

- Buy on Amazon
- Find on Goodreads

Further Information for *Why Fish Don't Exist*

If you loved *Why Fish Don't Exist*, check out more information about the book and its author:

- Visit Lulu Miller's website
- Read/Listen to an interview with Lulu Miller and NPR
- Listen to a podcast interview with Lulu Miller from Radiolab
- Read more about the cladists and how fish don't exist on Business Insider

The Stats:

Why Fish Don't Exist: A Story of Loss, Love, and the Hidden Order of Life by Lulu Miller
Published April 14, 2020 by Simon & Schuster
240 pages (hardcover)

Where to Find It:

- Buy on Amazon
- Add on Goodreads

CHAPTER TWELVE:
CONGRATS!

Congratulations! If you've gotten to the end of this template, you've written a substantive, informative book review that any visitor will be happy to read. You've connected your readers to valuable information and thoughtful critical discourse. From here on, you can replicate the same experience by going through the 7-step review template for further reviews. As you grow into a more confident book reviewer, you can decide which sections you definitely want to include and even add in more components you've thought of and enjoy writing.

APPENDIX A:

COMPLETED BOOK DISCUSSION GUIDE REVIEW FOR *CITY OF GIRLS*

Introduction for *City of Girls*

Elizabeth Gilbert, best known for her memoir *Eat, Pray, Love* (2006) and self-help book *Big Magic* (2015), returns to fiction with *City of Girls* (June 4 2019, Riverhead). This epic historical novel is told from the perspective of Vivian Morris, who moves to New York City when she is nineteen. Vivian finds community living in her bohemian Aunt Peg's midtown theater. But Vivian makes a crucial mistake that shatters her new life just as America enters the Second World War. *City of Girls* has received much acclaim. The novel was chosen as <u>Amazon's Best Book of the Year So Far in June 2019</u> and was nominated for a Goodreads Choice Award for Historical Fiction (2019). <u>The film rights</u> have also been purchased.

This book discussion guide contains spoilers

Plot Summary for *City of Girls*

In Elizabeth Gilbert's 2019 historical fiction novel, *City of Girls*, our narrator is 89-year-old Vivian Morris. In the opening pages, we learn that Vivian is writing to another woman named Angela. Vivian is attempting to answer Angela's question about who Vivian was to her late father. Vivian begins her letter in response by immersing us in her youth, starting when she moves to New York City at the age of 19 in 1940. Having been kicked out of college, Vivian lives with her bohemian Aunt Peg, who owns a vaudeville-style theater in Midtown Manhattan called the Lily Playhouse with her business and romantic partner, Olive. Vivian enjoys the glamorous life of the showgirls she befriends, in particular her roommate Celia, and experiences nights of excess, gluttony, and sexual pleasure. By day, she crafts beautiful costumes for the Lily using material from a fabric emporium where she strikes up a friendship with Marjorie, the quirky daughter of the store's owners.

As the Second World War begins to break through Vivian's sheltered life, Edna Parker Watson, an English stage actress and friend of Aunt Peg and Olive, becomes stranded in New York as England gets into the war. Aunt Peg puts on a show called "City of Girls" to feature Edna with the help of Billy, her husband who lives in L.A. "City of Girls" is a success with critics and audiences alike, and the cast and crew narrowly survives Billy's extreme behavior.

In March of 1941, tensions between Edna and her husband Arthur erupt during a fateful night, and Vivian is caught in a threesome with Arthur and Celia. Olive manages to keep Vivian's name out of the press coverage of the scandal, but the damage is done. Edna scolds Vivian, telling her she isn't an interesting woman, and Vivian flees the city, getting a ride home with her responsible Navy recruit older brother, Walter, and a fellow soldier who has a car available. On the way home, Walter lectures Vivian, and the unnamed soldier calls her a "dirty little whore," a remark that fills Vivian with shame and self-hatred as she lives at home with her parents in a state of depression. Vivian escapes a marriage to Jim Larsen, an employee at her father's company, because Jim enlists in the military after the Pearl Harbor attacks in December 1941.

Vivian senses that she's dodged a bullet and a life of unhappiness with Jim. When Aunt Peg drives up to her parents' house and asks Vivian to return to the city in the summer of 1942, Vivian eagerly hears her out. Aunt Peg's been commissioned to put on shows at the Brooklyn Navy Yard and needs a costume designer. Vivian agrees and, with delight, moves back to the Lily. Life has changed, with Edna on Broadway, Celia gone, and Billy elsewhere. Vivian dives headfirst into the creative obstacle of creating costumes despite war shortages. Vivian is distraught when she finds out Walter died on a ship in the Pacific.

After the war, Vivian and Marjorie purchase a house and set up a bridal gown boutique. Marjorie has a son who Vivian helps to raise, and Vivian finds sexual satisfaction in multiple male partners, though never a lasting relationship. When the Brooklyn Navy Yard is set to be formally closed down in 1965, Aunt Peg is asked to put on one last show. Since Peg is too weak from illness, Vivian agrees to take on the project. After the performance, a scarred police officer comes up to her and makes a stunning confession: he was the soldier who drove her to her parents' house and judged her to be a "dirty little whore." The man's name is Frank and he unsuccessfully attempts to apologize for the regretful words that have haunted him since, Vivian shuts him down and leaves. Seeking sympathy from Aunt Peg, Vivian is surprised when Peg expresses disappointment in her. Olive tells Vivian she needs to stand in the "field of honor" and take the high ground. After much deliberation, Vivian reaches out to Frank. Together, they strike up an unusual friendship that borders on a platonic romance.

Since Frank's PTSD makes him uncomfortable inside and can't bear physical touch, they walk through the city during long nights. Vivian helps him process some of his trauma. He eventually introduces her to his daughter, Angela, the woman to whom Vivian is writing. Vivian designs Angela's wedding gown in 1971. Frank dies of sudden illness in 1977. When Angela writes to Vivian, it's to tell her that her mother has passed away and that she was always curious about Vivian's close relationship with Frank. In closing, Vivian offers her friendship to Angela, looking back on her long and mostly happy life with extraordinary women.

Discussion Questions for *City of Girls*

1. *City of Girls* takes its title from the name of a play that the Lily puts on to great success. How do you interpret the title as a larger theme in Gilbert's book?
2. How does Vivian's late grandmother influence the woman Vivian becomes?
3. In many ways, Vivian's life is driven by a desire for pleasure. What are the potential consequences and dangers she faces in her pursuit for pleasure? How is her unconventional drive for pleasure indicative of the wider trends of liberation for women during the century?
4. Why does Vivian participate in the threesome? What events drive her to such a betrayal?
5. Discuss the theme of shame and gender in *City of Girls*. How does Frank's dismissal of Vivian as a "dirty little whore" inform Vivian's personal sense of shame? How do her views change over time?

6. How does the war give Vivian a sense of perspective? In particular, how does her brother Walter's death affect Vivian?
7. Define Olive's "field of honor" concept. How is Vivian's willingness to stand in the field of honor a rite of passage? How is her character different before and after doing so?
8. Discuss Vivian's evolving definition of emotional and physical intimacy. How do her earliest romantic and sexual relationships compare to her later relationship with Frank?
9. Vivian, her friends, and her colleagues embrace a radically unconventional lifestyle far ahead of their time. Vivian notes to Angela: "With the greatest of pride, I was able to look out across all the cultural upheavals and transformations of the 1960s, and know this: *My people got there first*" (p. 470). Discuss some of the ways that Vivian and her allies anticipated the century's revolutionary changes.
10. Vivian places a great deal of importance on female friendship and closes her narrative by offering friendship to Angela. Compare and contrast the friendships she has with women over the years.

Important Quotes from *City of Girls*

- "She was of the mind that people should make their own decisions about their own lives, if you can imagine such a preposterous thing!" — Vivian (referencing Peg), page 45
- "I hope you're having a good time, too. People will tell you not to waste your youth having too much fun, but

they're wrong. Youth is an irreplaceable treasure, and the only respectable thing to do with irreplaceable treasure is to waste it. So do the right thing with your youth, Vivian — squander it." — Billy, page 152
- "*'Hush,'* she said. "I'm thinking at the top of my lungs." — Peg, page 157
- "In my experience, this is the hardest lesson of them all. After a certain age, we are all walking around this world in bodies made of secrets and shame and sorrow and old, unhealed injuries. Our hearts grow sore and misshapen around all this pain - yet somehow, still, we carry on." — Vivian, page 342
- "Resist change at your own peril, Vivian. When something ends, let it end." — Peg, page 353
- "Anyway, at some point in a woman's life, she just gets tired of being ashamed all the time." — Vivian, page 377
- "The field of honor is a painful field...(It) is not a place where children can play. Children don't have any honor, you see, and they aren't expected to, because it's too difficult for them. It's too painful. But to become an adult, one must step into the field of honor. Everything will be expected of you now. You will need to be vigilant in your principles. Sacrifices will be demanded. You will be judged. If you make mistakes, you must account for them. There will be instances when you must cast aside your impulses and take a higher stance than another person - a person without honor - might take. Such an instance may hurt, but that's why honor is a painful field." — Olive, page 405
- "The world ain't straight. You grow up thinking things are a certain way. You think there are rules. You think

there's a way that things have to be. You try to live straight. But the world doesn't care about your rules, or what you believe. The world ain't straight, Vivian. Never will be. Our rules, they don't mean a thing. The world just happens to you sometimes, is what I think. And people just gotta keep moving through it, best they can."
— Frank, page 428

Pros and Cons of *City of Girls*

Pros

Pro: Vivian's conversational, dishy narration

Vivian narrates her story with candor and a sense of intimacy with the reader. She gives herself fully, admitting her deepest mistakes and sharing gossipy rumors and facts. She has a natural talent for writing who is able to look back on her life and shape it into a story laced with suspense, intrigue, conflict, and tension. This makes the pages fly by as you can't wait to hear what she'll tell you next.

Pro: Vivian is a flawed character who feels relatable

At the story's beginning, Vivian is 19. For the first time ever, she's allowed to explore her interests and her sexuality when she moves to New York City. Anyone reading *City of Girls* can relate to Vivian for her enthusiasm and her flaws. Gilbert's novel distills our universal tendency to make mistakes. One of its core themes is youth and how being young can lead to some immature errors that are hard to let down. When she hurts, we hurt, too.

Pro: *City of Girls* is rich with historical detail

Gilbert clearly did her research. The novel is packed with historical details that make you feel immersed in Vivian's life in New York City starting in the 1940's and through the decades that follow. Yet the setting never feels like you're reading a dense history book. Instead, Gilbert makes it come alive with just enough detail to feel like you're escaping present day.

Pro: *City of Girls* is a love song to anyone who has ever felt like a misfit

One theme in *City of Girls* is how Vivian connects with other misfits. In this sense, "misfits" means anyone who doesn't conform to society's rules. Vivian doesn't fit in because she's a pleasure-seeking young woman kicked out of college with no interest in marriage. Other characters Vivian meets, including Marjorie and Aunt Peg, reject norms of gender and sexuality. Together, Vivian and her friends create a found family that thrives on love and acceptance.

Pro: The book balances fun with heavy themes

City of Girls could have been a great beach read in its own right. But Gilbert's breezy novel is elevated by sincere, thought-provoking themes. The novel deals with heavy subject matter, like shame and trauma, that linger long after the final page has been turned.

Cons

Con: The novel is almost too long

As entertaining as Vivian's narration was, the novel felt bloated at times. Gilbert could have dramatically condensed the story while at the same time, the story would have benefitted from being spread out in Vivian's life post-WWII. *City of Girls* could have stood to lose a few pages early on.

Con: The "mistake" Vivian made was not convincing

Readers start out knowing that Vivian makes a mistake that dramatically changes her life; it's right there in the book's official description. Yet the way the threesome is written is slightly confusing. Did Vivian truly want to engage in the act? Her motivations weren't quite spelled out enough to make it believable that Vivian actually wanted to partake in the ménage à trois.

Overall Assessment for *City of Girls*

Elizabeth Gilbert's *City of Girls* is epic in scope, covering a large part of the latter half of the twentieth century. The novel sweeps readers off their feet with a captivating narrator who isn't afraid to admit her blunders. Written as a letter to an old friend, *City of Girls* is told in heroine Vivian Morris's confessional style, hooking readers with her storytelling skills, flawed and relatable characters, and glamorous life.

While the story is engrossing, some parts could be condensed while others would do better to be given in more detail, in particular when she summarizes several decades in just a few pages while devoting hundreds of pages to the events of a few days. Additionally, the book could have benefited from further clarification around Vivian's motives during her mistake.

However, despite these misgivings, the novel is ultimately a success. Vivian is such an entertaining narrator and captivating character in her own right that it's hard to put the book down.

It's easy to escape into Vivian's story in this character-driven historical novel that deals with topics like feminism, judgment, and youth. Just when you might think that Vivian is too frivolous a narrator, Gilbert proves that this is no gossipy book without substance. *City of Girls* rises above being just a quick beach read by handling heavy themes like trauma and shame.

Bottom Line: An unputdownable story told by a captivating, flawed character makes Elizabeth Gilbert's *City of Girls* a must-read for historical fiction fans and those who love stories with flawed-yet-relatable characters.

Similar Books for *City of Girls*

Dear Mrs. Bird by A.J. Pearce (2018)

City of Girls immerses readers in World War II and the mass mobilization of citizens to support the soldiers on the battlefield and those on the home front. Readers who enjoy Vivian's young perspective on the war will like A.J. Pearce's *Dear Mrs. Bird*. This novel is set in London during the early years of the war and is similarly anchored in the life of a young woman trying to make sense of the impossible conflict she and her country face.

Exit the Actress by Priya Parmar (2011)

Love the focus on drama and theater in *City of Girls*? Liked the historical setting? Try Priya Parmar's *Exit the Actress*. This novel also explores the world of acting. *Exit the Actress* is told through the eyes of Ellen "Nell" Gwyn, a real-life actress who rose to fame in Restoration England. An epistolary novel,

Exit the Actress is told in playbills, gossip columns, diaries, letters, and more mixed formats.

Sweetbitter by Stephanie Danler (2016)

Tess, the complicated heroine of Stephanie Danler's novel *Sweetbitter*, also arrives in New York in her early adulthood. Quickly taking a job at an upscale restaurant, Tess, like Vivian in *City of Girls*, makes mistakes as she matures. One of the most palpable feelings of *City of Girls* is how it feels to be young, a quality that *Sweetbitter* shares, making it of interest for readers who were moved by Vivian's blunders and successes both.

Warlight by Michael Ondaatje (2018)

City of Girls is as much about the lingering trauma of war as it is about living in the moment of the war. Readers who were intrigued by the aftereffects of World War II will find much to like about Michael Ondaatje's *Warlight*, which is set in London immediately after the end of the military conflict. Like *City of Girls*, this engrossing novel features a young protagonist trying to make sense of his fractured life post-World War II.

Further Information for *City of Girls*

Loved *City of Girls*? Take your reading to another level with these resources for fans of Elizabeth Gilbert's *City of Girls*:

- Visit Elizabeth Gilbert's website
- Read an exclusive excerpt of the novel on *O the Oprah Magazine*

- Check out an interview with Gilbert about *City of Girls* and her routine
- Browse book reviews of *City of Girls* collected on Book Marks
- Watch a video of Gilbert being interviewed about the novel

The Stats:

City of Girls by Elizabeth Gilbert
Published June 9th, 2020 by Riverhead (Penguin Random house)
480 pages (hardcover)

Where to Find It:
- Buy on Amazon
- Find on Goodreads

APPENDIX B:

COMPLETED BOOK REVIEW FOR *WHY FISH DON'T EXIST*

Introduction to *Why Fish Don't Exist*

NPR science reporter and podcaster Lulu Miller offers an eye-opening look at the way nature connects us all in *Why Fish Don't Exist: A Story of Loss, Love, and the Hidden Order of Life* (April 14, 2020, Simon & Schuster), her first book. Miller focuses on David Starr Jordan (1851-1931), a leading ichthyologist who specialized in fish taxonomy. Miller weaves Jordan's story of resilience after setbacks along with her own personal struggles following challenges. Along the way, Miller scrutinizes Jordan and re-evaluates her hero worship for the influential scientist, who played a substantial part in the eugenics movement in America. Ultimately, in trying to find order in her personal chaos, Miller delivers novel ways to see our natural world.

Summary and Key Takeaways of *Why Fish Don't Exist*

Lulu Miller opens her book *Why Fish Don't Exist* with a tantalizing question: how did scientist and educator David Starr Jordan (1851-1931) find the resilience to pick up and keep going after the 1906 San Francisco Earthquake destroyed his life's work?

And so kicks off Miller's debut as she introduces her personal story into her biography of Jordan. Jordan's courage to continue on after the earthquake smashed thousands of his fish samples was extraordinarily appealing to Miller, all the more so because the natural disaster shattered the glass specimen jars, leaving the fish unidentified.

As the book goes on, Miller summarizes Jordan's life and work as she fleshes out her own story. Miller struggled with depression over the years and clung to Jordan as an example of finding the courage to go on. But the more Miller investigates Jordan, the more complicated her relationship to him becomes as she learns the extent to Jordan's power. In particular, Miller unveils how influential Jordan was in the American eugenics movement and dangles a tantalizing rumor that he might have murdered Jane Stanford with poison.

Miller asks readers to question everything we know about nature and the hierarchies in life in her closing pages, challenging us to rethink the taxonomies that can be so harmful. Miller's life story, initially introduced to frame Jordan's biography, eventually emerges as the dominant narrative. Miller invites readers into her life as she heals from depression and finds self-acceptance and love.

Key Takeaways

- David Starr Jordan (1851-1931)was an influential naturalist and educator who specialized in ichthyology, the study of fish. Jordan was responsible for discovering thousands of fish, over a fifth of all fish species in his lifetime.
- Jordan might have been involved with the murder of Jane Stanford, the co-founder of Stanford University where Jordan served as president.

- Jordan endorsed the eugenics movement and was responsible for its spread in America, which led to thousands of government-sanctioned sterilizations.
- The theory that "fish" don't exist belongs to cladists, whose classification system is based on evolution. The cladists allege that the category of "fish" actually belongs to several different types of creatures since life evolved out of the ocean, so "fish" as we know it, encompass too many different species who eventually evolved.
- *Why Fish Don't Exist* is the debut book by Lulu Miller is a science journalist who has written with NPR and other publications like *The New Yorker*.

Pros and Cons of *Why Fish Don't Exist*

Pros

Pro: Miller's storytelling skills make her personal narrative a satisfying read

Miller's personal character arc is set alongside Jordan's but eventually eclipses his story to tell her own. Miller is a talented storyteller who pulls us in with honesty and self-scrutiny. The ending builds towards a satisfying climax that marries Miller's personal awakening with heeder revelations about Jordan, a man she once worshipped as a hero.

Pro: *Why Fish Don't Exist* is a lively, funny trip through the science of nature

Miller manages to balance the serious subject matter with the funnier or more light-hearted passages. Miller brings a needed sense of humor to the story that spurs readers on, never dragging down the narrative.

Pro: Miller's sense of curiosity about the subject is infectious.

You might pick up Miller's book and have no idea you're looking at a delightfully entertaining story that travels through the annals of history and braids multiple subjects, like natural science, psychology, true crime. Somehow Miller manages to pull it off and craft a fascinating story.

Pro: The book is short and never dense

If you're looking for a quick nonfiction read, *Why Fish Don't Exist* is for you. At 195 pages, Miller's can be read in one big gulp or over a weekend. The story never sags but races right along with great pacing.

Pro: Kate Samworth's stunning illustrations make Miller's story come alive

Each chapter starts off with one of artist Kate Samworth's captivating illustrations for *Why Fish Don't Exist*. This exquisite artwork is worth the price of the book alone.

Cons

Con: At times, Miller's explanations of scientific beliefs can be muddled and unclear

Sometimes when Miller is explaining a complicated scientific theory or belief system, such as the fact that fish don't exist, readers might struggle to understand them. Perhaps some tables or diagrams would have helped.

Overall Assessment of *Why Fish Don't Exist*

Lulu Miller's debut book *Why Fish Don't Exist* is a must-have book for anyone who likes reading about science, history, and psychology. Readers are in for a treat as Miller follows hunches and anecdotes down the rabbit hole, sparking a contagious curiosity for the subject matter in a manner similar to writers Mary Roach, Jill Lepore, and Susan Orlean. Miller mostly translates her topic well, though it can be challenging to follow at times when readers could have benefitted from more clear descriptions.

Miller's lively narrative breathes fresh scrutiny into her hero-worship for David Starr Jordan, a man whose myth she dismantles. Kate Samworth's breathtaking illustrations make this book a treasure to keep and look at again and again. Best of all, Miller successfully layers her subject and her personal story in a reckoning until they all come together in a cathartic ending.

Bottom Line: Lulu Miller's exciting debut, *Why Fish Don't Exist*, illuminates the natural order of life on our planet in this engrossing trip through science, history, and psychology threaded through with Miller's personal awakening.

Further Information for *Why Fish Don't Exist*

If you loved *Why Fish Don't Exist*, check out more information about the book and its author:

- Visit Lulu Miller's website
- Read/Listen to an interview with Lulu Miller and NPR
- Listen to a podcast interview with Lulu Miller from Radiolab
- Read more about the cladists and how fish don't exist on Business Insider

The Stats:

Why Fish Don't Exist: A Story of Loss, Love, and the Hidden Order of Life by Lulu Miller
Published April 14, 2020 by Simon & Schuster
240 pages (hardcover)

Where to Find It:

- Buy on Amazon
- Add on Goodreads

APPENDIX C:

30 BOOK DISCUSSION QUESTIONS

A list of 30 generic discussion questions
you can tailor to your book review.

For any book:
1. Analyze the title of the book. Why do you think the author chose it?
2. The book you're reviewing might include quotes, phrases, and books at the beginning of the book, otherwise known as epigraphs. If your book does have an epigraph, ask readers to analyze its significance.
3. What are 2-3 major themes in the book and how are they represented?
4. Take a look at the last paragraph and final lines of the book. How did you feel about the way the book ended? Was their closure? Did it leave you wanting more?
5. If the book has illustrations: how does the artwork impact the story?
6. Pick a quote that resonates with you. Why were you drawn to these words in particular?
7. If you could have anybody read this book after your recommendation, who would it be? Who needs this book in their life and why?
8. What was your first reaction to the book after finishing it?
9. Did your feelings towards the book change as you read it?

10. What questions would you ask the author?

For fiction:

1. How would you describe the personality of each main character in the story?
2. What do the main characters want at the beginning of the book? Why can't they have it?
3. If the novel were a movie, who would you cast to play the main characters?
4. How do the main characters change — or do they stay the same?
5. Discuss the characters. How did your opinion or reaction to them change throughout the story?
6. Which character did you identify with? Why do you think you connected to them?
7. Where do you project the characters to be three months after the ending? Six months? A year?
8. Do you feel this book's story was driven by its characters or its plot?
9. In what ways did this story make you reflect on your own life?
10. If you could choose an alternate ending, what would it be?

For nonfiction:

1. What did you learn from this book?
2. Has this book changed the way you see the world?
3. Discuss some of the ethical questions the book raises.
4. What other topics would you like the author to write about?
5. How did the author balance storytelling with stating the facts?

6. Sometimes the author will include themselves in the book, known as narrative nonfiction. If this book's author was part of the story, was it successful?
7. What information surprised you?
8. Which passages of the book were the most compelling?
9. What parts of the book did you Google to learn more about?
10. What lingering questions does the book leave you with?

BONUS:

HOW TO RECOMMEND BOOKS: A CRASH COURSE IN READER'S ADVISORY

Ever wonder how to recommend books? My love for giving people book recommendations led me to pursue my Master's of Library Science. I just loved connecting readers with great books, and the thousands of hours I spent reading, researching books, and browsing sites like Goodreads prepared me for this task. It felt like my calling.

When I learned the art of recommending books had a name — reader's advisory — and that you could actually study it, I was sold on library school. After taking some reader's advisory courses, along with writing about books here on the blog and professionally, like at EBSCO NoveList, I started to develop theories of my own about how to give book recommendations. I wasn't too happy with the fundamentals of reader's advisory taught in the classroom, so I created some personal reader's advisory theories. Now I get to recommend books in Book Riot's Tailored Book Recommendation (TBR) service.

This post is written for anyone who wants to learn how to recommend books to others. All sorts of people give book recommendations: book bloggers, bookstagrammers, book tubers, librarians, the Match Book column writers in the New York Times Book Review, and more. This is my intro guide, my practical crash course in reader's advisory, to help them and you get better at crafting awesome book recommendations that will keep readers coming back for more book talk.

Tip 1: Match feelings first

One of the core tenants of textbook reader's advisory is to match books on "appeal factors." These appeal factors break down a book's appeal into categories like Pacing, Writing Style, and Setting and are based on the idea that readers love the feel of a book.

However, you'll note that this approach doesn't reflect the way a book makes a reader feel. This, in my reader's advisory practice, is the core misconception about how reader's advisory is done. Reader's advisory theory has it backwards.

What bookworms read for is something that goes beyond their favorite genres, authors, and themes. The books they live to read, love, and cherish are books that make them feel something powerful, that knock them over with "The Feels," that vague-yet-specific emotional experience that all readers recognize, something that dislodges the mundane daily existence we live in and transports you to a powerful emotion, one that makes you feel alive and connected to the human experience.

To give great book recommendations, you'll want to match readers to books that give them similar "Feels." It's first and foremost about the emotional experience of reading an amazing book.

The Feels, in my opinion, cross favorite genres, comfort zones, and other places where reader's get stuck, mired in their safety net of familiar titles, authors, and genres.

OK, so that's all well and good, but how does that actually apply in book recommendations?

The first question you'll want to ask someone if they request a book recommendation is: "What was the last book you enjoyed, and why did you like it so much?" Listen to the cues they give you.

Someone might talk about a book they loved and say, "I just couldn't put down" – keywords for an engrossing story that brought them viscerally into the narrative. This is a code for a reader who likes to experience great stories. They are likely a bookworm who reads for escapism. You want to recommend a book that gives a similar feel: a terrific story, one that you yourself got sucked into so much that the events of the novel felt like they were a part of your life.

Or they might say, "I just loved the characters" or "I cried at the end." This reader might be looking for more books about a character's journey. They want protagonists who feel real, people who are flawed, relatable, but admirable, too, with convictions, personality, and a strong voice. Quick: What 3 fictional characters from books you've read in the last year would you invite to a dinner party? The characters you remember should give you a hint of a book you could recommend with similarly strong characters.

You can see in my list of book recommendations for fans of Donna Tartt's The Goldfinch that I break down the different appeals the novel might have for someone, including how it made them feel.

I also want to quickly say that intellectually moving books can be emotional experiences, too. A nonfiction book can reveal new things about the world that affects the way you feel, tell a story that is riveting and exciting, and draw on emotions to gut you with The Feels just as much as a novel. It's a myth that The Feels only come from fiction. What we connect to most as readers are stories, ones that grab us by the heart and mind.

Tip 2: Endorse books you love

One rule of recommending books you can't go wrong with is to endorse books you yourself love. Your greatest "reader's advisory ammo" are books that gave you The Feels, that you couldn't stop reading, that you won't shut up about and recommend to everyone with a deep sigh and a "Trust me, it's so good." I chalk this up to the Code of Good Books, a pact we enter into with other readers based on mutual trust and respect for another's reading opinions. We've all had those conversations with another reader—could be someone close to you or even a complete stranger you bond with at the library or bookstore—where you bond over the love of a good book.

Readers trust other readers. Recommending books you've loved means readers will bank on your enthusiasm and the magical Code of Good Books.

Above all, we trust each other to not steer the other wrong, and how can you do that if you're recommending books you know you can talk up in an endorsement backed by your personal experience? When others recommend a book to me I'd otherwise not take a chance on, I trust their enthusiasm. Time and time again, I'm glad I've picked up a book I wouldn't have dreamed of reading if it wasn't for the endorsement of my friends, family, and colleagues, including the book blogger and Goodreads world. Right now, can you think of books that people have recommended that you were skeptical of at first but ended up loving?

Sometimes, of course, it won't work out. Your recommendation just won't click with someone else. To every book, its reader. Let it go and move on. Ask them about their favorite recent reads. Don't take it personally, and know that readers trust your good intentions above all else. Nobody actually goes around facetiously pushing bad books in others' hands. That's against the Code of Good Books that we all abide by.

Also, recommending books that you've already read helps ensure you won't put a troubling book in the hands of someone who raised specific trigger warnings. I don't have a problem with recommending books I haven't read, but if a reader notes that they don't want books with offensive content, worrisome themes, and anxiety-inducing topics, I go out of my way to only recommend books that I've read and can verify do not contain triggers. If I get stuck, I consult a friend who's read a book I'm considering recommending but haven't read myself. I take content triggers seriously and so should you.

Here I want to address a topic you've probably wondered about: to recommend or not to recommend books you haven't read. A lot of librarians and readers make the mistake of thinking that it goes against Book Law to recommend a book if you haven't read it yourself. That's just not true. Unless you read hundreds of books each year, there will always be books you haven't read but have heard on good authority (from friends, colleagues, book world people, Goodreads reviewers you follow) are decent.

I have my limits and personal rules about recommending books I haven't finished myself, but the main one is that the majority of books I recommend in a bunch must be ones I've read some or part of. Note I said "part of": This is a good reason to try to read the first chapter of each book you check out of the library or buy. You can tell a lot from a first chapter: voice, pacing, what the "hook" is to get you to keep reading, whether the setting is evocative, and so on. Plenty to go off of when recommending a book.

Tip 3: Look beyond books

I love books. You love books. The reader you're recommending to loves books. We all do. But there's also media we enjoy outside literature. Next time you're recommending a book, ask your reader about what other kinds of entertainment they enjoy.

Ask the book lover you're recommending about other media they love. Find out their favorite TV shows, movies, podcasts, and music. Ask them what kind of stories they love beyond books.

You're recommending books, sure, but you might also be recommending based on how they like to be entertained. To practice, think about a movie, TV show, magazine article, or other type of storytelling media that you've recently enjoyed. What do you love about the story? The characters? The plot? The topic? The suspense? The visual style? The setting? Jot down a few ideas for book recommendations based on this non-literary art.

Want an example? Check out my post on the blog about books for fans of Netflix's Mindhunter, and my book recommendations for Veep and Succession (two HBO TV shows) on Book Riot show how to pull apart what makes a show appealing and translate that into similar books.

Tip 4: Include diverse picks

It's 2020, and publishing is still suffering from a lack of diversity. Despite gains and progress, it's still possible to recommend books by authors privileged enough to be in the majority. However, as a book recommender, you can have a big impact and influence on how many more diverse voices get read.

As a book recommender, you're in an influential position to help connect readers with books by diverse writers. Use it.

Try aiming for at least one or two good diverse picks in a list of book recommendations. Balance male authors with female, trans, and gender non-binary writers. Highlight international writers. Pick writers whose voices reflect minority and underrepresented cultures, religions, and diasporas. That includes economic and regional diversity. Look for books that are written by or feature differently abled characters. Don't automatically assume that a romance pick needs to be between a man and woman but offer books that include queer courtship, love, and relationships, too.

Tip 5: Throw a wild card in there

At the end of the day, you can never be positive about the books you recommend, even if they seem like iron-clad sure bets. That's why I advocate for including a wild card pick with your recommendations.

If you've got a hunch that someone might like a book, even if there's no proof to point to, you've got to go with your gut and trust your intuition. Have confidence in yourself. You know a good book when you see one. Yes, you do!

Take a chance and recommend something wacky, weird, or wonderful. If you only ever end up recommending safe choices, you'll never grow as a book recommender. And who knows? You could be connecting someone with their new favorite writer, book, or series.

BONUS:

20 BOOKISH WEBSITES TO FIND YOUR NEXT READ

I'm writing this list of the best websites about books for me five years ago. Back then I was deep in the beginning of learning about the book world and would have welcomed a list of the great book websites to help me learn what to read next. Getting to know the publishing industry is a lifelong process of book discovery, and the Internet makes the literary community more accessible and inclusive than ever.

These 20 book websites (plus a few extra way down at the end) are the places I go to find out about new books being published, to deepen my understanding of literature and reading, to get book recommendations, to grapple with critical book reviews, and more. I hope you'll find your next favorite book through this list of great book websites to grow as a reader.

(1) Amazon Book Review

Visit: https://www.amazonbookreview.com

Love it or hate it, but Amazon is a quality place to go to find out about new books. The Omnivoracious Amazon Book Review is a flagship for good book content, with recommendations from celebrities and other notable readers being a unique feature. I love the author interviews they have on their site, with writers like George R. R. Martin, Holly Black, and Charlie Jane Anders recently stopped by for a chat, often on the podcast. Amazon's Best Books of the Month list is one I check religiously for new books to add to my TBR. They often surprise me with little-known reads I wouldn't otherwise have on my radar (even if I think they make YA an afterthought), which is why I rate them highly for "new book discovery," meaning a place where you can learn about books to read.

Strengths: Author interviews, previews of new releases, lists of recent award winners, podcast, new book discovery

(2) Book Bub

Visit: https://www.bookbub.com/welcome

When BookBub first came on the scene about five years ago, I signed up for their signature daily newsletter with hot deals on eBooks. I scored a lot of great books to load up my Kindle, but I didn't really follow the site for a few years as I wasn't reading too much on my eReader. Now they're everywhere, moving beyond the email list to create original bookish content. It's now totally expected to have one of their many comprehensive book lists pop up in a search for new books. The only downside that I see is that now you have to have an account to view their book lists or other blog content. I do like how they track book recommendations from authors like Stephen King, Jill Shalvis, and Nora Roberts.

Strengths: Book list articles, book recommendations, eBook deals, new book discovery

(3) Book Marks

Visit: https://bookmarks.reviews

One of the sites associated with Literary Hub or "Lit Hub," which I write up as #12 below, Book Marks is *the* place to go if you want to find book reviews of the latest big books. Book Marks' specialty is aggregating adult literary fiction and nonfiction book reviews and then assigning them a score card so you can see how many reviewers gave the book a Rave, Positive, Mixed, or Pan. Without a doubt, if you want to find out the critical consensus on a book before buying it or checking it out of the library, Book Marks should be your first stop. I also like how the site regularly interviews book critics to ask them more about their bookish lives. The site also reprints classic book reviews.

Strengths: Book reviews, coverage of new books, literary criticism, book news, essays

(4) Book Riot

Visit: https://www.bookriot.com

Sure, I might be a little biased to include Book Riot in my list of the best book websites since I write for them, but the fact is, Book Riot is one of the leading destinations on the web for book lovers and certainly one of the top best sites for new books. Book Riot's got all areas of the reading life covered and does an especially good job at highlighting diverse authors, featuring all genres, and amplifying thoughtful and at times controversial opinions about books, publishing, and reading. The annual Read Harder Challenge pushes readers beyond their comfort zone with categories like "A book by an AOC (Author of Color) set in or about space" and "A novel by a trans or nonbinary author," and a thriving community of challenge takers trade book recommendations and ideas. Book Riot's many book podcasts are also must-listens for readers wanting to learn about new books and what to read next.

Strengths: Diversity, essays, book list articles, all-genre coverage, podcasts, book news, reading challenge, new book discovery

(5) Brain Pickings

Visit: https://www.brainpickings.org

Looking for engrossing essays about books that will push you emotionally and intellectually? You'll definitely want to stop by Brain Pickings, the literary love child of Maria Popova, a blogger who decided to create an "inventory of the meaningful life" more than a decade ago and share it with other readers. Popova's one-woman show is an intensely personal exploration of art and ideas, with coverage of children's literature alongside philosophy, literary fiction, and creativity. Sign up for her newsletters to get a hit of thought-provoking writing a few times a week, guaranteed to break up your mundane day. Popova is author of two books: *Figuring* (2019), which highlights the hidden legacy of influential female thinkers, scientists, and creators, and *A Velocity of Being: Letters to a Young Reader* (2018), a book for younger readers that collects essays about reading from leading creative thinkers like Neil Gaiman, Shonda Rhimes, Ursula K. Le Guin, and Elizabeth Gilbert.

Strengths: Literary criticism, essays, backlist coverage, newsletter

(6) Bustle Books

Visit: https://www.bustle.com/books

The website Bustle is designed for the modern woman, and the ample literary coverage on their standout Bustle Books channel reflects that. Here readers will find profiles and interviews with female authors, lists that focus on feminism, and personal essays that explore the experience of being a female reader in today's world. Bustle Books is known for provocative articles challenging the publishing world to be more diverse and more female inclusive. You'll also find fun articles, too, about books, TV and film adaptations, and books in pop culture.

Strengths: Feminism, diversity, essays, book list articles, all-genre coverage, new book discovery

(7) CrimeReads

Visit: https://www.crimereads.com

Like Book Marks, CrimeReads is a branch of Literary Hub (discussed in #12 below). This book website has a niche focus on "crime" in literature: through true crime, mysteries, thrillers, fiction about crimes in general. On CrimeReads, you'll find essays about writing and reading crime fiction, appreciation of and interviews with crime fiction authors both well-known and underrated, reading lists for crime fiction and nonfiction, and coverage of crime in TV, movies, and other media. CrimeReads also has essays and original reporting on true crime. If you're a mystery and thriller lover, appreciate a good courtroom novel, or just love reading about true crimes stories, you'll definitely want to head over to CrimeReads and marathon read their quality content.

Strengths: Mystery/thriller/suspense, true crime, nonfiction, the writing life, book list articles, essays, literary criticism, new book discovery

(8) Electric Literature

Visit: https://www.electricliterature.com

With its signature tagline of "Reading Into Everything," Electric Literature hosts an eclectic mix of bookish coverage, ranging from highbrow literary criticism to horoscopes for writers and everything in between. A hallmark of Electric Literature is a focus on reading more diversely, and a regular feature called Read More Women asks writers to recommend books by women (a response to male authors who only recommend books by fellow male authors). One thing I love about Electric Literature is how often they touch on writing and the life of being a storyteller. Electric Literature also publishes original fiction in its literary magazine, so keep your eyes peeled for some of today's best authors and new and emerging voices alike converging there.

Strengths: Literary criticism, diversity, essays, author interviews, the writing life, all-genre coverage, book news, book list articles, new book discovery

(9) Epic Reads

Visit: https://www.epicreads.com

Oh, Epic Reads: what started as an arm of HarperCollins publishing house has turned into the go-to destination for YA book fans. Readers of young adult literature love Epic Reads for the humorous tone, creative article ideas (bookish horoscopes, fan reactions to plot twists, book title or song lyric? challenges, etc.), addictive quizzes, and, of course, the many TBR-exploding lists. You'll also find book trailers, cover reveals, and details on the latest books and tour dates for YA authors. Even though Epic Reads is part of HarperCollins, they don't only put the spotlight on books through their publishing house. Epic Reads is simply and purely about celebrating YA literature, no matter whose imprint is stamped on the book jacket. So often YA can be a heavy genre, with books tackling serious themes, but Epic Reads always reminds me that reading (*and* YA) can and should be fun, too.

Strengths: Young Adult (YA) books, quizzes, book list articles, new book discovery

(10) Five Books

Visit: https://www.fivebooks.com

Five Books has a niche formula and does it well: a list of five great book recommendations. This powerhouse book website solicits a fascinating mix of today's most interesting, creative, and thoughtful "Experts" —like Mary Beard, Madhur Jaffrey, Mia Farrow, and Jo Nesbø—to offer five book recommendations on a specific topic, such as "The Best Prose Poetry," "Congress," and "Zombies." An additional nice feature of Five Books is the ability to make your own lists and share your expertise. The site lives up to its tagline of "The Best Books on Everything" as you'll find as wide a variety of book lists and book coverage as anywhere on the web.

Strengths: Book list articles, book recommendations, new book discovery

(11) Goodreads

Visit: https://www.goodreads.com

In the 9 years that I've been a member of Goodreads, I've seen the site change a lot—for the better. Goodreads is perhaps the most essential website for readers as it allows you to track the books you've read, want to read, and are reading and add custom shelves to sort books. Connect with other readers in groups and follow authors for updates and exclusive information. The Goodreads lists are a rabbit hole to tumble down and find out more about books. I've found that the user-generated reviews have also improved over the last few years, going from one-line snarky hot takes to more thoughtful reviews. Plus they are home of the popular Goodreads Reading Challenge, an annual self-challenge to set a goal of how many books you want to read that year. Even the Goodreads blog is getting better at publishing creative articles about the bookish life.

Strengths: Community, reading data tool, book list articles, user-generated reviews, reading challenge

(12) Largehearted Boy

Visit: http://blog.largeheartedboy.com

Largehearted Boy is a book and music blog established in 2002 by David Gutowski and an essential corner of the literary internet. Obsessed with best-books-of-the-year lists? Make sure you bookmark Largehearted Boy, which compiles an index of the best-of lists you can peruse till your heart's desire. Also great for book discovery is the weekly "Books of the Week" that Montreal bookstore Drawn & Quarterly hosts on Largehearted

Boy. What I love about Largehearted Boy is the thoughtful and honest book reviews, the blending of music and literature with the "Book Notes," where an author matches a mixtape to their new book. Like Brainpickings, Largehearted Boy traces a very personal experience of inquiry into being a reader, writer, listener, and human being to provoke our own consideration. It's an honor to share in it.

Strengths: Book list articles, author interviews, essays, book reviews, new book discovery

(13) Literary Hub (a.k.a. "LitHub")

Visit: https://www.lithub.com

The parent site of the aforementioned Book Marks and CrimeReads, Literary Hub pumps out new book content for readers on the daily. I also suggest signing up for the LitHub newsletters as they come out each day with a summary of new posts not just on LitHub but elsewhere on the Internet. The weekly edition is a must-read, too, and it's where I get many of the interesting bookish links I post on the Facebook page for my blog. On LitHub, you'll find an endless stream of great writing about books, including essays on writing and reading, author interviews, highbrow intellectual literary criticism, book lists, and new fiction. Browsing LitHub is like reading a digital version of a literary magazine (like *The New York Review of Books*) that you actually want to read. LitHub's specialty is literary fiction, though they do also cover various genres, too. However, you likely won't find much YA and children's literature coverage on LitHub, excluding when they come up in personal essays about reading or writing kidlit.

Strengths: Literary criticism, literary fiction, nonfiction, essays, book list articles, author interviews, new book discovery, book news

(14) The Millions

Visit: https://www.themillions.com

Established in 2003, The Millions is one of the oldest book websites around, and over the past 15 plus years it has built up a reputation for being a gathering point for intellectually curious readers. Head over to The Millions if you want to check out the latest buzzy literary releases, hear more from authors about how they conceptualized and wrote their new book, discover the most anticipated books published in the month ahead, and find out what books were nominated for awards. The strength of The Millions is definitely literary fiction and nonfiction. Two of the best recurring features on The Millions are the annual Year in Reading, in which notable creatives and thinkers share a little about their year in reading, and The Millions' Most Anticipated: The Great First-Half Year 20XX Preview, a TBR-toppling list of the most anticipated books of the year. This list comes out in two parts: January for the First-Half and July for the Second-Half. You'll want to comb through these articles with your TBR ready, and you can find all The Millions lists on Goodreads for easy record keeping. I look forward to them every year as traditions, almost holidays, on the bookish calendar.

Strengths: Literary criticism, literary fiction, nonfiction, essays, author interviews, book list articles, previews of new releases, book news

(15) *The New Yorker*'s Books Section

Visit: https://www.newyorker.com/books
Visit The Page-Turner Blog:
https://www.newyorker.com/books/page-turner

Arguably the best literary magazine in America, *The New Yorker* is also a flourishing website with tons of great book content, most of it found on The Page-Turner blog. On *The New Yorker*'s Books channel, book reviews, publishing news, essays and articles from the magazine about writing and literature, and *New Yorker* staff book recommendations. Note that you'll need a subscription to view more than a few articles a month. I admit I'm a proud subscriber of the magazine; I never recycle the issues, and they take over every corner of the house like an invasive species, but I wouldn't have it any other way!

Strengths: Literary criticism, essays, literary fiction, nonfiction, author interviews, book reviews, book recommendations, book news

(16) *The New York Times Book Review* Online

Visit: https://www.nytimes.com/section/books

It would hardly be a list of the best book websites without including *The New York Times*' Book section. After all, *The New York Times Book Review* is one of the most prestigious and influential periodicals in publishing, and landing a coveted spot on its bestseller lists is just about every writer's dream. Fortunately, the *Review*'s virtual presence is a worthy digital companion to the supplement you'll find in Saturday's paper. Online, you'll get the same great book reviews, essays, and humor sketches, plus some podcasts going inside the *Book*

Review and publishing that week that are seriously worth checking out. Every week I look for the New & Noteworthy feature, which highlights new releases you should put on your radar, and the Editors' Choice: New Books We Recommend This Week, a weekly list that includes extracts from the critics' reviews that'll make you want to read these fresh books. One of my favorite recurring series in the *Book Review* is the By the Book interviews with writers, thinkers, and creatives, which discuss the bookish life and always includes interesting books to add to your TBR. You can find all of these digitized and uploaded weekly.

Strengths: Book reviews, book recommendations, author interviews, literary criticism, book news, podcasts, previews of new releases, new book discovery

(17) NPR Books

Visit: https://www.npr.org/books

National Public Radio (NPR) has always been ear candy for readers, but now you can get all their great book programming online in one spot. The NPR Books site collects all the author interviews, book reviews, and stories about the reading life that you'll get on the radio. If you've ever had the experience I have where you've gotta turn off the car in the middle of a story and you don't have a pen or paper ready to record a book title or author name, they've got you covered. Beyond audio programming, NPR Books has a solid stream of book reviews and feature articles about writing and reading with a focus on diverse authors. Breadth and depth of coverage is a signature of NPR, which is why you'll find articles about children's books alongside graphic novels and comics and highbrow literary fiction. NPR Books is known for one more thing: the annual end-of-the-year book concierge. This behemoth of a book recommendation machine is a slick book discovery tool to find more than 300 of the best books of the year. Yes, I said 300. I've found so many great books this way, ones that were otherwise overlooked in best-of-the-year lists, and the methods to sort by what you're in the mood for make this giant list manageable, with some seriously high-quality UX. Oh, yeah: you'll be working through that list for the rest of the upcoming year.

Strengths: Book reviews, diversity, book list articles, author interviews, book news, all-genre coverage, new book discovery

(18) Publishers Weekly

Visit: https://www.publishersweekly.com

If it's publishing industry news you want, Publishers Weekly should be your first stop. Publishers Weekly (PW) is packed with insider-y gossip-y content about what's hitting the shelves now and soon. Writers will want to check out PW's articles to get an idea of what agents are buying and what trends are moving through books. I also sometimes mine the announcements that publishers make of new and upcoming books to get ready for upcoming releases and add them to my calendar.

Strengths: Book news, publishing industry information, book list articles, previews of new releases, new book discovery

(19) Read Brightly

Visit: https://www.readbrightly.com

Kid lit fans, this one's for you. Read Brightly is an online children's literature website that's part of Penguin Random House. Read Brightly is an excellent resource for readers of children's literature and the adults who help children learn to love reading. One great feature of this website is the way each article is broken down by reading levels, a key distinction that takes the guessing game out of trying to connect children to the most age and reading level appropriate books. A flurry of articles celebrate kid lit, with creative and diverse book lists around categories like "Move Over, Rover: 10 Picture Books That Feature Unusual Pets." Each month, Read Brightly hosts a reading challenge for kids designed to help them stretch themselves and discover new books. Like Epic Reads, this book website is hosted by a publishing house but features books from all parts of the children's literature publishing world. Read Brightly truly lives up to its motto "Raise Kids Who Love to Read" as that passion for literacy and raising bookworms comes through in every story they write.

Strengths: Children's literature, Young Adult (YA) literature, book list articles, previews of new releases, reading challenges, all-genre coverage, book discovery

(20) Tor

Visit: https://www.tor.com

Last but definitely not least, Tor is the go-to destination for science fiction and fantasy readers on the literary web. Tor has long published books, but their online presence takes their mission to highlight great voices in speculative fiction and pushes it further, creating a space for a community of SFF fans to grow and thrive. On Tor, you'll read honest book reviews that are fair and critical of the books and authors in question, original fiction, lists of books, personal essays, eBook deals, SFF industry news, and coverage of SFF-related media, like *Game of Thrones*. What I like about this site is the freedom that Tor gives its bloggers and staff writers to really speak their minds about books. You might find articles about super-super niche sub-sub-sub genres you didn't even know were a thing, but you definitely won't find BS here. This makes Tor a leading place to go for readers who want to dig into the issues behind books.

Strengths: Science fiction, fantasy, SFF related TV shows and movies, book news, book reviews, essays, book list articles, book discovery

More great book websites

Here are a few other book websites you'll definitely want to check out but didn't make the full list (because I ran out of time!):

Atlas Obscura's Books Section: https://www.atlasobscura.com/categories/books

Catapult: https://catapult.co

Flavorwire Books: http://flavorwire.com/category/books

The New York Review of Books: https://www.nybooks.com

Vox.com's Books Section: https://www.vox.com/books

ACKNOWLEDGMENTS

Thank you to my family for their support.

ABOUT THE AUTHOR

Sarah S. Davis is a freelance writer, editor, and book content and marketing strategist based in the Philadelphia area. Sarah's writing about books has appeared on Kirkus Reviews, where she also served as a copywriter and production editor, as well as Book Riot, Electric Literature, Audible, Psych Central, EBSCOHost, BookRags, and many more. In 2014, Sarah started Broke by Books, a book blog whose guiding mission is to spread a contagious love for reading and help grow an inspired, engaged, and fearless reading life.

Sarah holds a BA in English from the University of Pennsylvania and a Master of Library and Information Science from Clarion University. In 2021, she earned her MFA in Writing for Children and Young Adults from Vermont College of Fine Arts.

When she isn't reading or writing, Sarah enjoys leaning into cat lady spinsterhood, illustrating, reading tarot, and seeing as many films as she can.

OTHER BOOKS BY THIS AUTHOR

Be sure to check out Sarah's quotation collections:

A Reader's Library of Book Quotes

A Purrfect Collection of Cat Quotes

Brave Brain: 365 Quotes about Hope and Healing for Mental Health Recovery

Her mental health guided journal:

The Tomorrow Journal

Her book trivia book with 500 trivia questions and answers about literature:

The Great Literature Trivia Quiz Book

And her guide to book blogging:

Book Blogging Hacks

Follow Sarah on Goodreads for the latest news: (https://www.goodreads.com/author/show/8152419.Sarah_S_Davis)

And be sure to stop by her blog, Broke by Books (www.brokebybooks.com)

Enjoyed This Book?

Please help others find this resource by leaving a review on Goodreads and Amazon.

Printed in Great Britain
by Amazon